D0460804

OUR *Love* IS HERE TO *Stay*

photography by KATHLEEN FRANCOUR

text compiled by DAVID & HEATHER KOPP

Our Love Is Here to Stay
Text Copyright © 2000 by Focus on the Family®
Published by Harvest House Publishers
Eugene, Oregon 97402

Focus on the Family, headed by Dr. James Dobson, is an organization
that reaches families with the message of God's love. Focus on the Family® is a
registered trademark of Focus on the Family, Colorado Springs, CO 80995.

For more information, please contact:
Focus on the Family
Colorado Springs, CO 80995
1-800-A-Family
www.family.org

Kathleen Francour's hand-tinted photographs reflect the old-fashioned
values of home, family, love, loyalty, and friendship. The photography in this book
is copyrighted by Kathleen Francour and may not be used without the permission
of the photographer. For more information, please contact: Kathleen Francour
Photography & Design, P.O. Box 1206, Carefree, AZ 85377.

Heather and David Kopp are the coauthors of *Love Stories God Told* and *Unquenchable Love*.

Library of Congress Cataloging-in-Publication Data

Kopp, David 1949 –
        Our love is here to stay / Focus on the Family ; compiled
by David and Heather Kopp ; photography by Kathleen Franour.
        p.   cm.
        ISBN 0-7369-0135-3
        1. Marriage Miscellanea. 2. Love Miscellanea. I. Kopp, Heather
Harpman, 1964 –   . II. Focus on the Family (Organization)
III. Title.
        HQ734.K677   2000
        306.81—dc21   99-44131
                                                                    CIP

Design and production by Koechel Peterson & Associates, Minneapolis, Minnesota

Harvest House Publishers and Focus on the Family® have made every effort to trace
the ownership of all stories, poems, and quotes. In the event of a question arising from
the use of a story, poem, or quote, we regret any error made and will be pleased to
make the necessary correction in future editions of this book.

Special thanks to those people who allowed us to share their love stories
and to the couples who posed for the photographs.

Scripture quotations are from the Holy Bible, New International Version®,
Copyright © 1973, 1978, 1984 by the International Bible Society.
Used by permission of Zondervan Publishing House.

All rights reserved. No portion of this book may be reproduced
in any form without the written permission of the Publisher.

Printed in Italy.

00 01 02 03 04 05 06 07 08 09 / PBI / 10 9 8 7 6 5 4 3 2

CONTENTS

FROM THE FIRST

"I Do"

Celebrating the Choice to Love

The happiest day of my life,

When, thanks to God, your low, sweet "Yes"

Made you my loving wife!

WILLIAM C. BENNET

Do You Love Me?

I got married 78 years ago to a wonderful man named Cecil. Back in 1922, dating was very simple—going to church and picnics into the country, holding hands. We'd go to the silent movie show for just ten cents. Our favorite show was a melodrama with the heroine strapped to the railroad tracks and the train a-coming.

After the date, Cecil would drive me home in his Model T touring car. I'll never forget the night that he looked at me and said, "I want to ask you something... Do you love me?"

I said, "Yes."

Then he said, "Will you marry me?"

And when I answered yes, he leaned over and kissed me for the very first time! But oh! That was worth waiting for!

JO MATRIED

My true love hath my heart,

and I have his,

By just exchange

one for the other given.

SIR PHILIP SIDNEY

Her sweet,

"I will" has made ye one.

ALFRED, LORD TENNYSON

The Little Details

My father is not a man to express feelings and emotions freely. He is also not one to remember an important event—or so I thought. On one occasion he told me something, something that showed the deep love and respect he has for my mother. A love and respect that touched my heart in a way I will never forget.

My dad and I were on the front porch of my parents' home. We happened to be watching all the grandkids on the front lawn when somehow the conversation turned to my parents' wedding day. My dad was so proud and yet tender as he recalled the day. He remembered every detail: the exact time he saw my mother, the color of her dress (this was 1952—big, flowy white gowns were not what most women wore), what she looked like, how he felt—all the little details that I didn't think he would have taken the time to remember. What a special moment to realize he had kept this picture in his heart all those years! What a blessing to see how much he loves her even to this day, 47 years later.

It is a joy to have my mom and dad as an example for my own kids, that as a marriage matures, love goes on.

LAURA KNUDSON

Surprised By Love

Well, well, how little a man understands himself or knows the future! The day I married her I was in mortal dread lest she should care for me too much and want to be affectionate and all that; and now here I am, hoping she will. Don't see as I'm to blame, either. She had no business to grow so pretty! When the color comes into her cheeks, and her blue eyes sparkle, a man would be a stupid clod if he didn't look with all his eyes and feel his heart a-thumping.

It's a scary thing, this getting married . . . . See where I am now. Hanged if I don't believe I'm in love with my wife!

E.P. ROE

He Fell in Love with His Wife

I came alive when I started loving you.

C.S. LEWIS

My dove in the clefts of the rock,
in the hiding places on the mountainside,
show me your face,
let me hear your voice;
for your voice is sweet,
and your face is lovely.

SONG OF SONGS 2:14

I Wish I Could Remember

The #1 rule for a good
marriage is the rule that
you are married.

AUTHOR UNKNOWN

I wish I could remember that first day,

First hour, first moment of your meeting me.

. . .If only I could recollect it, such

A day of days! I let it come and go

As traceless as a thaw of bygone snow;

It seemed to mean so little, meant so much;

If only now I could recall that touch,

First touch of hand in hand—Did one but know!

CHRISTINA ROSSETTI

I never saw so sweet a face
    As that I stood before.

My heart has left its dwelling place
And can return no more.

JOHN CLARE

"First Love"

Let the wife make

the husband glad to

come home,

and let him make

her sorry to see

him leave.

MARTIN LUTHER

A successful marriage requires falling in love many times,

always with the same person.

MIGNON McLAUGHLIN

WITH EACH

Tender Kiss

Cultivating Kind Affection and Romance

Affection is responsible for nine-tenths

of whatever solid and durable happiness

there is in our natural lives.

C.S. LEWIS
The Four Loves

Love, the gift of life,

A Kiss, the gift of Love.

AUTHOR UNKNOWN

There is no more lovely, friendly and charming

relationship, communion or company than a good

marriage.

MARTIN LUTHER

Is not a kiss the very autograph of love?

HENRY FINCK

Let him kiss me with the kisses of his mouth!

SONG OF SONGS 1:2

Saying Love

I've been married 53 years. During the first 15 years of my marriage, my husband rarely ever said he loved me. I knew he loved me, but I often felt sad that he didn't *say* it. Then one day he came in the house with a handle that he had made for my broken spatula. I hadn't even asked him to do this. I looked at him and finally realized this was his way of saying love.

You see, love doesn't have to be expressed in words; it can be in gifts and little things that you do for one another, as simple as a home-baked pie or a new handle for your broken spatula.

HELEN TRAVIS

KISSES: *Words which cannot be written.*

NICOLE LOUISE DIVINO

I may grow old, but my heart

will never grow tired of

loving you.

AUTHOR UNKNOWN

O happy hours when I may once more encircle within these arms the dearest object of my love…when I may again press to my heart which palpitates with the purest affection that loved one who has so long shared its undivided devotion.

ALEXANDER HAMILTON RICE

Love Notes in the Kitchen

The last day of January, my wife Edith and I celebrated our forty-fifth wedding anniversary. I never dreamed that a couple could be so happily married at our age.

I've always loved my wife but was often very thoughtless of her. For example, I'm a perfectionist, and I expected the house to be in order all the time, even when we had three or four small children.

Then changes began to take place. I can remember a time when the sink was full of dirty pots and pans. Instead of criticizing my wife, I wrote love notes and placed them in the bottom of each pot and pan. That went over so well that I was inspired to begin helping her, often surprising her, by doing housework when she was out.

One time I was finishing the dishes when she arrived home, and in her cute, sweet way she asked, "And what do you think you're doing?" I responded, "Oh, I'm just loving my wife."

SIDNEY ALDRICH

Love is an endless act of forgiveness, a tender look which becomes a habit.

PETER USTINOV

Husbands ought to love their wives as their own bodies.

He who loves his wife loves himself.

EPHESIANS 5:28

It is the passion

that is in a kiss

that gives it its sweetness;

it is the affection

in a kiss

that sanctifies it.

CHRISTIAN NESTELL BOVEE

O love! O fire! once he drew

With one long kiss my whole soul through

My lips, as sunlight drinketh dew.

ALFRED, LORD TENNYSON

Now a soft kiss—Aye, by that kiss, I vow an endless bliss.

JOHN KEATS

He is a creature of vision

and she is a lover of touch.

By a little unselfish forethought,

each can learn to excite the other.

DR. JAMES DOBSON

In *Laughter*
AND IN *Tears*
Growing Stronger Through Troubled Times

Fair or foul—on land or sea—

Come the wind or weather

Best or worst, whate'er they be,

We shall share together.

WINTHROP MACKWORTH PRAED

There is no more lovely, friendly,

and charming relationship, communion,

or company than a good marriage.

MARTIN LUTHER

Rich in Love

I was married in 1929 in Chicago. I'll never forget how awful it was during that depression time. There were breadlines. There were men out of work all over, selling apples on the corner, begging, and nobody had any money, nobody could get a job.

My husband was laid off right after we were married, and I got pregnant, and we all had to go home to my mother. My dad was working, but he made only eighteen dollars a week. Yet this drew us all together, and it especially drew my husband and me together. There were times when he'd look at me and I'd look at him, and we'd say, "What are we going to do?"

But the Lord just took care of us every moment. We didn't have much, but we had our love for each other, which strengthened day by day.

ELSIE HOYER

Something Good

In our pursuit of marital oneness, we must never permit failure or disappointment or tragedy to rob us of our confidence... No situation is so desperate that God's grace is not sufficient. Building a Christian marriage begins with a conscious confidence that a determination to live for God will result in something good.

DR. LARRY CRABB

[Love] always, always trusts,

always hopes, always perseveres.

Love never fails.

I CORINTHIANS 13:7,8

A Legacy of Love

Mrs. Eleanor Woods, my grandmother, is happily anticipating the arrival of her eleventh great-grandchild. For her, it all began one summer evening when Grandpa proposed to her on the porch of her mother's home.

Though my grandfather isn't with us any longer, before he died he and Grandma had celebrated their fiftieth anniversary. I asked my grandmother recently about the secret to a long-wedded life. She said she thought the most important thing was to remember that each partner should share in the give and take, to be careful to share in compromise. She also believed in commitment to her wedding vows.

In the thirty-seventh year of their marriage, my grandfather suffered a massive heart attack. Though he did not die, he was not able to do many things for himself. My grandmother cared for him every day for 13 years until the end. She told me that she had promised to be with him "in sickness and in health, until death do us part." She was faithful to that promise, and she has passed on to her children, grandchildren, and great-grandchildren a wonderful legacy of love and tenderness.

KIMBERLY MOORE

Together

How happy am I, having you at my side,

Through life's ever changeable weather;

My hopes and my fears unto you I confide,

As we move heart in heart on together.

We have tasted success, we have drank of desire,

With hearts light and gay as a feather;

And the day and the deeds that our spirits inspire—

We have lived and enjoyed them together.

Through care and misfortune and trouble and pain,

Made part of life's changeable weather,

And sickness and sorrow came once and again,

We met and endured them together.

So together still sharing what fate has in store,

May we go to the end of our tether;

When the good and evil things all are shared o'er,

May we share the last sleep still together.

HUNTER MACCULLOUGH

Love alters not

with his brief hours and weeks,

But bears it out

ev'n to the edge of doom . . .

WILLIAM SHAKESPEARE

The Most Wonderful Thing

The most wonderful of all things in life, I believe,

is the discovery of another human being

with whom one's relationship has a glowing depth,

beauty, and joy as the years increase.

SIR HUGH WALPOE

Married life is a marathon, not a sprint. It is not enough to make a great start toward long-term marriage. You will need the determination to keep plugging on, even when every fiber of your body longs to quit.

DR. JAMES DOBSON

Young love is a flame; very pretty,

often very hot and fierce, but still only light and

flickering. The love of the older and disciplined heart

is as coals, deep burning, unquenchable.

HENRY WARD BEECHER

Beauty and love
   are all my dream

they change not
   with the changing day.

Love stays forever
   like a stream

that flows
   but never flows away.

ANDREW YOUNG

I love thee with all the breath,

smiles, tears of my life.

ELIZABETH BARRETT BROWNING

Tie a Knot

My husband and I have been married 38 years, and we had a lot of problems.

But we are so glad we stuck it out! So when I see people having problems, I like to share this

motto of mine: "If you feel like you're at the end of your rope, tie a knot and hang on!

Because God is a God of miracles, and He's holding the other end."

PAT HICKS

We have lived and loved together

Through many changing years;

We have shared each other's gladness

And wept each other's tears,

And let us hope the future

As the past has been will be;

I will share with thee my sorrows,

And thou thy joys with me.

CHARLES JEFFREY

No Matter What

My husband and I have been married almost 39 years. Our wedding ceremony took place at my hometown church, an Episcopal church, and when our priest counseled us in 1952 before the wedding, he told us that the secret of a happy, successful marriage is not to let a day go by without saying "I love you," whether you mean it or not at the time.

So we've done this, and those words have seen us through raising two children; a near business failure; learning to pray together (that was really something hard!); the complete destruction of our home, two cars, and our house trailer in a fire storm; and also my husband's brain tumor, which he miraculously recovered from. It's amazing what those three words can carry you through.

Don't misunderstand me. The happy times are wonderful, and we always want the happy times. But it seems that the tough times are the ones where we even draw closer to one another and where we really look at one another and say, "This is it. I love you and I'm sticking by you, no matter what."

MARY MANN

EVER *Deeper,* EVER *One*

Growing Closer to God and Each Other

Love is not a matter of counting the years...

but making the years count.

MICHELLE ST. AMAND

Though weary, love is not tired;

Though pressed, it is not straitened;

Though alarmed, it is not confounded.

Love securely passes through all.

THOMAS A KEMPIS

Grow Old Along With Me!

The best is yet to be,

The last of life, for which the first was made:

Our times are in his hand

Who saith, "A whole I planned,

Youth shows but half; trust God: see all,

Nor be afraid!"

ROBERT BROWNING

The fullest glory in marriage comes when two

people…trust God to lead them through His ultimate

curriculum of love and righteousness. The marriage

will not be perfect, but the partners will be

experiencing the very best of both journeyes.

MAERRITA TUMONONG

If ever two were one, then surely we,

If ever man were lov'd by wife, then thee.

If ever wife was happy in a man,

Compare with me, ye women, if you can.

ANNE BRADSTREET

Quiet Time

I was married 52 years. When my husband and I had been married 42 years, we both retired and I found I needed some private time so I kept getting up earlier and earlier in the morning to be by myself. The problem was that each time my husband got up too—right when I did.

Finally, I got up at one-thirty in the morning and I turned around, after I was sitting down at the dining room table, and there in the living room was my husband. He said, "Where's the coffee?"

So I said, "We've got to have a talk."

I told him I had to have some private time to keep my sanity. I said I would like to have two hours and I would prefer to have from four to six in the morning. If he would let me have that private time, with no phone calls, no demands on me for anything, I would bring him coffee in bed at six o'clock.

He said, "It's a deal." So then I was able to devote the other 22 hours a day to his health and happiness. About six months before he had his stroke and passed away—that was ten years later—I asked him, "How do you rate our marriage, on a scale of one to ten?"
He said, "Well, I think it's got to be a ten, because I don't know anybody happier."

So I think that my having private time and our arranging things this way added a great deal to our happiness.

JANET OVERHOLSER

Saying "I Love You"

My parents have been married nearly 50 years. What makes
their marriage last? When I ask them, they usually smile and say
they don't know. But I know. In hundreds of wonderfully ordinary
ways, they've done what it takes to stay in love.

They've gone on several vacations for two—no kids allowed.
They hold hands when they pray at the dinner table. They believe
that a commitment to each other is a commitment for life.
They do things together, and they do things separately.

Dad washes the dishes on Sunday morning, to give Mom
more time to get ready for church. Mom asks Dad's opinion
about her new clothes. They both enjoy a good baseball game,
time with their grandkids, and dinner out together.

They tell each other's stories. They worry over each other's
health. They send each other sappy birthday cards.

And they still get a little shy when they talk about how
they met and fell in love.

In all these things and more, they've shown me what
saying "I love you" really means.

BARBARA SHERRILL

O, my love is like a red, red rose,

That's newly sprung in June:

My love is like a melodie

That's sweetly play'd in tune.

So fair thou art, my bonnie lass,

So deep in love am I:

And I will love thee still, my dear,

Till a' the seas gang dry.

Till a' the seas gang dry, my dear,

And the rocks melt wi' the sun:

And I will love thee still, my dear,

While the sands of life shall run.

ROBERT BURNS

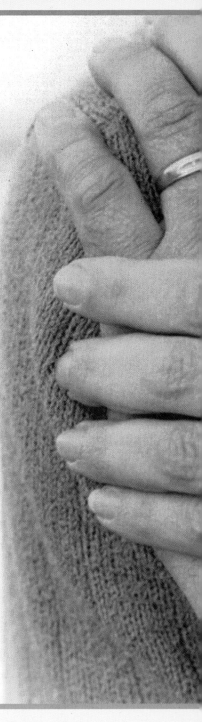

Just Between You and Me

We are now reaping the benefits of the kind of long-term marriage where the bonding between two people is so thorough and so intense that the line that separates the two of you is blurred. It's an exclusivity; it's a relationship that flowers and grows through the years. It was cultivated in youth; it was watered through time, carefully maintained, and now it comes into maturity.

DR. JAMES DOBSON

Above all else, guard your heart for it is the wellspring of life.

PROVERBS 4:23

Ever Together

I have now been married ten years. I know what it is to live entirely for and with what I love best on earth. I hold myself supremely blest—blest beyond what language can express; because I am my husband's life as fully as he is mine. No woman was ever nearer to her mate than I am: ever more absolutely bone of his bone, and flesh of his flesh. I know no weariness of my Edward's society: he knows none of mine, any more than we each do of the pulsation of the heart that beats in our separate bosoms; consequently, we are ever together. To be together is for us to be at once as free as in solitude, as gay as in company. We talk, I believe, all day long: to talk to each other is but a more animated and an audible thinking. All my confidence is bestowed on him, all his confidence is devoted to me; we are precisely suited in character— perfect concord is the result.

CHARLOTTE BRONTË

Jane Eyre

Daily Tokens

To cultivate joy in marriage, we look for
God at work in the one we love. His
fingerprints are everywhere: in that
wedding ring, scratched, but irremovable;
in the wildflowers gathered for the dinner
table; in the swelling voice in the shower,
off-key but enthusiastic; in the mended
clothes, the repaired appliance, the
toddler's hurt finger healed with a kiss.
When we turn our attention to what's
good and precious in our home, when we
search out and appreciate the beauty of
marital love in its daily, earthy tokens, we
gather God's treasure, one jewel at a time.

PAUL THIGPEN

In Spite of Me

I am lucky to have my wife. I was drawn to her by her
Christ-centered life and now, 49 years later, I still worship her.

You see, my own make-up is that I am a negative, cynical guy and,
as you guess, not a joy to live with.

In spite of me, she is gentle, loving, and so faithful in serving
our family and church. I have to say that the Lord blessed me through
my beloved. I have prayed the Lord would take me before I ever betrayed
my wife, whose life is lived for me and with me.

RICHARD STASIOR

Upon my life there lies the print of a woman's palm, rosy, soft, and tender—ah,
my Heart, you know whose hand it is! Day by day I have felt it, continually leading
me upward, smoothing down the roughness in my nature, and teaching me to live.
As much as I am more than I might have been, I owe to that kindly hand.

M. REED

Love Letters of a Musician

Home

"Where's home for you?"
a stranger asked a fellow traveler.

"Wherever she is,"
came the reply, as the man
pointed at his wife.

ROBERT FULGHUM

Overheard Conversation

A Recipe for Marriage

My maternal grandparents were married for 59 years and lived in Odessa, Missouri,

which is a farming community about 30 miles east of Kansas City. The Kansas City newspaper

once sent out an investigative reporter in search of a formula for their marital happiness.

He noted that they had a lot in common. Each of them did outdoor work on the farm, and they

ate plain cooking and they slept from nine to five. Yet, each one of them exhibited independence

of opinion. My grandmother said that "you make adjustments for disagreements," and my granddad

said that he didn't know much about the recipe for a great marriage but, "she makes good

buttermilk biscuits each morning and that's why I stuck with her."

My grandmother was endowed with a great deal of wisdom. "When things go wrong,"

she said, "the least that's said, the less we had to regret." Another favorite was, "It's best not to

resent and then have to repent." Now that was back in the late thirties, before psychiatrists

and marriage counselors were prevalent. But as you can see, my grandparents

didn't have much need for them anyway.

"Though our bodies with age and labor are feeble and very much bent,"

my grandma once wrote, "may God help us be content."

KAREN HARMON

AS LONG AS

We Both

SHALL *Live*

Treasuring Each Other Through Time

I love thee, I love but thee

With a love that shall not die

Till the sun grows cold

And the stars grow old.

WILLIAM SHAKESPEARE

Simple Actions and Quiet Faith

During my growing up years, I don't remember seeing my parents kiss. But although they weren't as openly expressive as some couples, they showed their love in a lifetime of simple actions and quiet faith. The first house my father built, he built as a wedding present for my mother. In turn, my mother left the sparkling city life she loved to follow a country boy to a small town on the Oregon coast. Instead of dinner parties and theater, they gleaned leftover crops for the food bank and took long walks every morning.

After 45 years of marriage, my father was diagnosed with cancer. As he neared the end of his life, it became harder and harder for him to go to church. Up to the end, my mother went as much as she could, and each time she did, the pastor looked at her during the prayer request time and asked, "How's Ray?" She would answer and the church would pray for him.

The week after he passed away, my mother and I went to service as usual. When the pastor asked for prayer requests, he didn't look my mother's way. Finally, my mother waved her hand at him and said, "Pastor, you didn't ask how Ray is today." After a long, awkward silence, he ventured, "Well, Helen, how's Ray today?" With a twinkle in her eye and hope nurtured by thousands of quiet hours together, she looked up and replied, "He's just fine."

BETTY FLETCHER

Nothing is more beautiful

than the love that has

weathered the storms of

life. The love of the young

for the young, that is the

beginning of life. But the

love of the old for the old,

that is the beginning

of things longer.

JEROME K. JEROME

Never Old

To me, fair friend,
you never can be old,

For as you were
when first your eye I eyed,

Such seems
your beauty still.

WILLIAM SHAKESPEARE

There is no recollection like that of loving,

for love itself is recollection,

and in loving one loves all the thousand memories

that store themselves away.

M. REED

For hearing my thoughts,

understanding my dreams,

and being my best friend...

For filling my life with joy

and loving me without end...

I do.

AUTHOR UNKNOWN

I can't re-enter April and my youth.

Gray though my head is now, love me today,

And I shall love you when your own is gray.

PIERRE De RONSARD

Meaningful Vows

When I was a child, I didn't have to worry that my parents would not be together.

They had a mutual love and respect for each other. My father was faithful to my mother and

to their marriage vows. Daily I was comforted by the fact that they did truly love one another.

My father saw my mother for the first time at the school bus stop. She had just

moved into the neighborhood and was a new student. My father can still recall their first

meeting, and I believe it was love at first sight. Their first date was a Sadie Hawkins dance. After

hearing stories of my dad as a young boy, I believe it was a good thing he met my mother

when he was older. All of the girls who knew him when he was younger couldn't stand him

because he liked to tease them unmercifully. Happily, he matured before my mother met him!

They dated through their teen years and married at age 20.

Their marriage has endured for 47 years. "Through sickness and health,

for better or worse, for richer or poorer, to love and to cherish, till death do us part"—

I have observed that those vows truly do mean something.

ELAINE YOUNG

The blood runs thinner, yet the heart

remains as ever deep and tender.

FYODOR TYUTCHEV

Last Love

Love in Old Age

It is love in old age, no longer blind, that is true love. For love's highest intensity doesn't necessarily mean its highest quality. Glamour and jealousy are gone; and the ardent caress, no longer needed, is valueless compared to the reassuring touch of a trembling hand. Passers-by commonly see little beauty in the embrace of young lovers on a park bench, but the understanding smile of an old wife to her husband is one of the loveliest things in the world.

BOOTH TARKINGTON

I love you ever and
ever and without
reserve. The more
I know you the more
have I lov'd....
You are always new.
The last of your kisses
was ever the sweetest;
the last smile the
brightest; the last
movement the
gracefullest.

JOHN KEATS

Love at the closing of our days

is apprehensive and very tender.

Glow brighter, brighter, farewell rays

of one last love in its evening splendour.

FYODOR TYUTCHEV